IN POETRY THAT DAZZLES with its erudition and cosmopolitan approach, Christina Pugh shows us the role of language in constructing—and eventually deconstructing—the self. "In a room made of windows, glass is the skin," she tells us. At turns luminous and devastating, the work in this gorgeous volume reveals every facet of the narrator's lived experience—from inhabiting the physical body to articulating a sophisticated artistic sensibility—as discursive constructs, arising out of a nexus of community and shared experience. "[L]ike a flock we all landed at Teresa and the angel," she recounts. Yet, at the same time, Pugh interrogates the narrator's lingering sense of cultural and linguistic otherness, revealing connection with those around her as both contingent and inherently unstable. The voice that emerges from this intersection of philosophy and art, celebration and elegy, is as singular as it is eloquent. "I'm thinking everyone must have a fulcrum," she writes, "The place from which we radiate." These are poems that radiate with incredible artistic vision and writerly craft.

RECENT AND SELECTED TITLES FROM TUPELO PRESS

THE RIGHT HAND

The Right Hand

Library of Congress Cataloging in Publication Data available on request
Cover and Text Design by Howard Klein
Cover Art: Gian Lorenzo Bernini, "The Ecstasy of Saint Teresa," 1647-1652, Cornaro Chapel,
Santa Maria della Vittoria, Rome, Italy.
First paperback edition October 2024.

Tupelo Press
P.O. Box 1767
North Adams, Massachusetts 01247
(413) 664-9611 / Fax: (413) 664-9711
editor@tupelopress.org / www.tupelopress.org

Tupelo Press is an award-winning independent literary press that publishes fine fiction,
non-fiction, and poetry in books that are a joy to hold as well as read. Tupelo Press is a
registered 501(c)(3) non-profit organization, and we rely on public support to carry out
our mission of publishing extraordinary work that may be outside the realm of the large
commercial publishers. Financial donations are welcome and are tax deductible.

This project is supported in part by an award from the National Endowment for the Arts

THE RIGHT HAND

Christina Pugh

T|P

TUPELO PRESS
North Adams, Massachusetts

ACKNOWLEDGMENTS

Grateful acknowledgment is made to the editors of the following publications, in which sections of *The Right Hand* first appeared:

Exilé Sans Frontières: "[Every pin is a tender path]"; "[All the nerve passageways crowd]"; "[Her hand moved slowly]"; "[thus   skin   is the portal]"; "[And skin   is an organ]"

Image: "[The church had other beauties]"; "[This faith was not mine]"

Notre Dame Review: "[When ruin is the deity]"; "[*I fell into the Baroque*]"; ["my first   photo of Teresa and the angel"]; "[*Can you touch   the statue* is what the man]"; "[the boy who holds the arrow is an angel and a girl]"; "[the angel's wing will   draggle its song will]"; "[a low tenor hymn   filled the altar and the near pews]"; "[Teresa's dress is topography   a country]"; "[I'm thinking everyone must have   a fulcrum]"; "[Teresa and the angel form an existential *happening*]"; "[On a cloudy day in the Santa Maria]"; "[But one light behind them is eternal   manufactured:]"

Ocean State Review: "[Her robe is an edge effect]"; "[Is it always a question]"; "[But doesn't every photograph]"

Plume: "[Maya Lin made a river out of pins]"; "[She said she saw her own veins]"; "[*To interrupt pain feedback loops*]"

The Plume Anthology 9: "[*Love looks not with the eyes, but with the mind.*]"

Grateful acknowledgment is also made to the American Academy in Rome for a visiting artist residency that allowed me to visit and to research *The Ecstasy of St. Teresa* (1645-52) by Gian Lorenzo Bernini in the church of Santa Maria della Vittoria in Rome.

My thanks to my family and friends for their support: Sybil Pugh, Wendy Jones, Lisa Petrie, Jason Roush, Jodie Hollander, and Harriet Melrose. Special thanks to the editors at Tupelo Press for believing in this book. My love and unending thanks to my husband, Rick DelVisco.

And my deepest thanks to the many practitioners of body-work who have assisted me with chronic pain over more than two decades. Your knowledge and care have made a difference in my thinking and in my life.

for Rick,
and for my mother

TABLE OF CONTENTS

I.

There is a needle
  Pulling a thread through your veins,
A needle pulling the sap
  From the root to the bole...

—Phillis Levin

The Chinese medical therapy that is probably best understood in the
West is acupuncture, the insertion of very fine needles into specific superficial
locations on the surface of the body. Described in Chinese medical literature as
harmonizing qì and xuè, acupuncture has been used for centuries to treat a
variety of disorders by restoring harmony of yīn and yang, qì and xuè.

—American College of Traditional Chinese Medicine
at California Institute of Integral Studies

INTO THE SKIN

From everything I understood:
Je vous suis, volevo dire. Languages
entwined in me, the braided
trunk of a tree begun in delicacy.
My body was still speaking into—
speaking against his fingers.
This is what I understood of long,
long pain within the body.

The true pain of longing—
of *yearning*, an archaic word:
No one yearns anymore, I'd heard
an ancient woman say. The cloud
and sunbeam of acute
verbal memory.

Love looks not with the eyes, but with the mind. And therefore is winged Cupid painted blind.

He would visit her body every night: *listen feel*: don't see.

She was not allowed to look at him, but underneath

his wing she was a blue morpho grazing.

Then she knew the colors not in nature,

psyche so sweet in the embedding.

You worked in a room with no windows.

In another room, called *Preservation*,

a woman named Africa

was sewing the ragged spine of a codex.

In a room made of windows, glass is the skin.

Every pin is a tender path.

Every arrow begins to sew.

The skin, not the mind, creates the soul.

All the nerve passageways crowd

Into a finger's whorl.

A nexus: metropolitan.

A city in a palm.

Her hand moved slowly   tectonically across my trunk

The other hand beneath my back   was cradled   an asymptote

West–East, east–west   a lower   premonition

Breathe with this I told myself   the wind

have done

As it is with the sun courting miles, or dimmest starshine—

Right ankle: left wrist. Tundra in between.

Epidermis   it's skylike

A name to harbor   galaxies

I know no nomenclature

for skin that sheathes an ankle,

how it differs (if it does)

from the skin that drapes

a shoulder's larger circle

but skin   is the portal

the laminate   the barrier

the reef against   the system

or lesser systematic   churn

What it may   conduct   I know

a harp   amid the tremors

And skin   is an organ

Aeolian   it bundles   strums

Vesuvian   it kindles

When pierced   it will   swarm

She said she saw her own veins

branching when she closed her eyes:

the eyelid's imprint like a cloth

crazed in cross-stitch. Or *thatched*,

I tried to think. Then closed my own

eyes to find my inner eyelid. It's not

very starry. It is not even color.

It's the closest my body

comes to the conceptual.

Maya Lin made a river out of pins.

The pins on the wall marked the Hudson's movements.

Like a battlefield, or a soul pierced by arrows.

When the pins clustered thickly, like *crescendo* in music—

This was where the wall was wounded deepest.

Every thumb   creates a bruise

the swath within   .   imagining a

wild   carrot   index   -   all the

dawning   pre-knowledge of the imprint

The tenderest   darts

like   nectar   in a gullet

irascible   journeying

exquisite   micro-dram:

a pencil pushed

so deep into my socket

Speaking of nails, I thought I'd said—

Little Dipper needles were

swirling round my left wrist

and crept against my forearm.

A woman named Wise had put them there,

and I had left her table with

pain etched in as intricate

as ragged cursive lettering

carved into bark. I looked for her

again, tethered by this cloud so

burning and ethereal…

it would be a pilgrimage, to find her.

This bracelet of nails

Around my wrist — an intergraft

Honeysuckle *chevrefeuille* deflect:

S'ils restent unis ils peuvent bien subsister

This tug is my lifeboat

This braid now my hand

The slow narcotic pins wove

a chain of heat   around my calf   like eyelets,

then fur   if the portholes in

the lace rubbed out

as if my heart were beating on

the skin   against my thigh

as if my heart draped   across

the region   below my hip to

sever   it there   as Giacometti

finally did: one leg   precariously

arched and balancing   sovereign

upon the thinnest   plinth

When you left the room

my leg already floated

its shooting stars radiating

kindly in space

Every pin that pierced it

was a star   in my firmament,

a blueprint only you

can see   and, in a sense,

imagine

When all the pins were in:—

I fell asleep and dreamed

that my foot had ten toes.

But I do have ten toes.

I just couldn't arrange them.

White like a page

White lie of a page

When I lay face down

you turned the pager on its edge

rested it against the berm

my smallest finger

formed and said: *If you*

get restless…and I loved

that little   rested edge

Anything sexual: it's why we close our eyes

We're always closing our eyes against beauty

This is what you find in a Bernini sculpture

Filling your vision as you circle around it

The ankle will swirl and the hair serpentine

I'm trying to recover a pathway to the body

My eye is filling for the love of doubling back

Everything escapes into a tree, unto metaphor

Consent is a power.

To yield is a power.

I might even say: *to yearn* is a power.

When I turned on my stomach

When you lifted one shoulder then replaced it

When you closed my fingers on the little

monitor   I couldn't   see you

I was more alone than ever

There was no separation between us

When you see the back of my body lying there

When you see my hair and not my eyes

Are you seeing   my right hand

Are you seeing the one who is stopping   by woods

Are you seeing the vein I can't   touch the cursive   capillary

To interrupt pain feedback loops, try writing with your non-dominant hand.

At night, I tried to write with my right hand.

My pen stubbed the paper, then trailed leggy

glyphs on squares. I copied lines, *Whose woods*

these are. And 1, 2, 3, 4: primary numbers.

The curviest letters were the hardest thing—

I skittered half a gambrel roof to try to end

an *h.* Such ungainly posture in my wilting

fingers as they trudged the weird

frontier of the page. My wrist had to

double back, sniffing with its snout:

:

Everything hurrying down to my right hand:

the wind inside my muscle   laborious exchange

the weight of every orphaned mark

Or letters   blown like

cherry   glass like elephant   petals

invisibly   thickening

:

This fullness   and emptiness

I recall   from being young   a liquid

skirmish   when I was instructed

to trace   the h

:

Ex voto

Ex vuoto

Six letters from the void

I feel them looking backward :

So many   renderings   of Orpheus   alle spalle

Reversing   the stitches on   the sewing machine

:

These notes I hear differently

Planed through my right hand

They belong to the birds

Who are entering stage left

:

And that blue   window I

fashioned   my mind into:

sculpted clean of everything

No moth   wing   no bird

:

But I need you   inside me

raking   this vernal pool

without you   there I'm all

alone   in my body

:

This roiling   hunger

The hole inside my trunk

Trying   to emanate from four   coordinates

And from there, I fell further

out of language.   In pain that had

no predicate: flat within

the night sky, I managed to ripple

a cocoon from inside my death.

It knit every plain and

valley in my skin. I was not

comforted, but understood

that gravity would

someday take me back.

It was not the (I was speaking

in public) *It was being*

pulled and hushed into

the terrifying colorless

river of the self

(they seemed to nod)

It was not dialing 911

Instead it was the tremulous

dissent and relinquishment

The letting go of qualities

The self now fallow

field against the sun

pensiero   pansement   *je pense donc je suis*

but who will I be   or   how

can I   follow

One foot in

"I met your father last night

He studied with *Adore*"

This troubled me, as the living

shouldn't   meet the dead   that way

Not that door   never yet

It's perilous   how we seam

And I saw a face I'd left behind

Vibrant in a photograph

She was mine   once   she would always be

The narrative of earlier   life a graven   image

The lilac–white   kidney shape

floated   when   I closed my eyes

its descent   was rhythmic:

Sisyphus   it rose again

the slightest   selvage at its edge

Pricked into the shoulder

blade   the kidney-

shape a   wing

might draw

against the skin

before it sprouts   angles

feathers of   itself

(think of   ink

written   on the skin

before surgery:

mine was blue   lightning

the doctor   scratched

above my hip)

the wings can't see they

multiply   a kite   lifting

above   a monarch swarm

with   pain the wing

will transfer furl   love

imparts   its blueprint:

the *germ* of the wing,   as Plato

said in *Phaedrus*:   when it

pierces   your shoulder   blade it

feels like cutting teeth, he said

Gold lamé

That   blade along   your back

The one   in the interior

My shoulders trace   a figure-eight

They   write against the air

      Lame was the word   I learned

to translate *blade* in French   Then heard

the *lame* of the   sun   could make

 a murderer

Just a little   poison: it's   the logic   of the vaccination

Pinpricks release   the cloudbursts   that will obfuscate

A mole of pain   an arcane   unit   of measurement my organism   working:

the miracle   of that…

a dim   homeostatic hum

to ratify   my organs' weight

a wing   nearly notional

The handle of the prayer-gong is

rough against my fingers

they smooth preternaturally

when closing   upon it:

its roughness makes my fingertips

untroubled in contrast, my unskilled

hand now a sort of glass....

my hand that may remember

how little it requires to make a sound

I am grateful for this instrument, its imperfections.

The sound it made was dissonant,

though it loved melody most.

It always needed sanding, tuning,

resin, even when I was young.

I'd looked to a flock above

A dotted flock of generic birds

I entered them severally

A compass briefly scattered

So an entity shapes what flies beyond it

And I landed in a rich pool

Swimming into character

A story mine and not-mine

A picture on an easel

Everything would be told, but not in words

II.

Beside me, on the left hand, appeared an angel in bodily form....In his hands I saw a great golden spear, and at the iron tip there appeared to be a point of fire. This he plunged into my heart several times so that it penetrated to my entrails. When he pulled it out, I felt that he took them with it, and left me utterly consumed by the great love of God.

—St. Teresa of Avila, *Life of Teresa*

Bernini created a sculptured picture of Teresa's Ecstasy, which was itself originally a mental picture as well as a powerful physical phenomenon.

—Howard Hibbard, *Bernini*

L'INCONTRO:
THE MEETING

The church had other beauties

but when the doors   opened

like a flock   we all landed

at Teresa and the angel

A woman was making   the sign of the cross

like blinking   like pushing

a lock of hair away

I asked my husband: *how   does it go*

do you cross from the left

shoulder right   shoulder what

I can't   remember he said   and tried both ways

Teresa   and the angel: two

incongruous   wings two

chambers   in an   anteroom

pierced by   rained   gold

This faith was not mine

this   bite   into colorless

this   flush with skin and bone

this eating   the circle   this

fingering of names   that

bridge of bending   angels

But it was an *incontro*   in Bernini's   Italian

a woman's   skin to be pierced   by an angel

a saint   exhaling   between two cuts   in marble

and coupling far   into the twenty-first century

When ruin is the deity

where tearing is ubiquity

the headless the fingerless

the wristless   presiding—

Bernini's   fulguration

brims in the periphery, its

marble bodies   unchipped

unamputated   always

and still   resplendent

in   their opening

I fell into the Baroque

was how I once put it:

I had loved   the broken

archaic   tender

and Byzantine slender—

but now the extravagant

fullness of surrender

held my mind   as if nailed

to that wonder

my first   photo   of Teresa and the angel:

a column intrudes like a left-hand margin

or the   ultra-authoritative   spine   of a book

the porphyry the marble   scripted in veins

it's a doctrine   —   it tells me

to yield is a power

Can you touch   *the statue*, is what the man

asked me   if I did, my hand would catch

in its angular   folds would   furrow

in their   conscious   irregular   water

would   bathe   in the scarcity

of sunspot   at Teresa's thumb

Is it always a question   of beauty in the offing

Teresa often called herself   a *mujercilla*

but Bernini worked   to enlarge   her skin

cohered   among the sexes   neither woman

nor man her   face amplified   to a plane   of reception

Her   head in a cradle her   head inlaid like wood

swaddled in concentric   radii   in pain

I wished neither to hear nor to speak

and her eyes are closed, so she wishes not to see

etymologies of trauma will   ferry the dream

from corona   thunder   to her tremoring   head

And yes, the head

derives from the body

her head ex-voto

broadened   to receive

On a cloudy day in the Santa Maria

people wander   in pairs or one by one

the gentled ripple of the light   a relief

slight smiles   a dreamier   air within the scene

And we seem to prefer   this cloudy   caress

this shallow lancination   of gray on the diagonal

.50 Euro in the slot will light Teresa—

someone pays it   then we all stand together

silently after the stagecraft   snuffs

But one light   behind them is eternal,   manufactured:

the sun in its linear   gilt   wood rays

everything   ether

Bernini made   tactile

and rain the extensor   of heaven,   with no drops

I'm thinking   everyone must have   a fulcrum

The place from which we radiate   divide and sublime—

so Teresa and the angel   work to form a gradient

The angel   plucks   not an inch

of her robe   His left arm reaching

for what animates her clothing   verses an amphora-

shaped window between them

that houses these electrons: *desire*   *to cleave*

Anything sexual   it's why we close   our eyes

I see that the angel's   face is incidental

They share no verbal flicker no

catch   within expression

only the riveted   blank gold arrow

The boy who holds the arrow is an angel and a girl

I feel him reaching for the pronoun *they*:

Their own folds love their skin, twirling ever closer

While five of their super-differentiated fingers

Curve incidental at Teresa's robed shoulder

Their one bare nipple and voluptuous neck

Are whispering now: *Give him the veil*

You must transpose the picture quite,
And spell it wrong to read it right;
Read him for her and her for him;
And call the saint the seraphim.

— Richard Crashaw

ambidextrous   dyslexic

which one's in the muscle   can you

number   the languages that

read from   right   to left

You can transpose the figures   from their capsule of pageantry

Put them on postcards with   imperial   plum backgrounds

This one comes a little   closer than my camera can

Her head   slightly reared

Her teeth   bared a little

And all the glottal   invisible   inside

A low tenor hymn   filled the altar and the near pews

like rain in swale   like barely   sloping hills it rose

a hum of Latin ambient   I couldn't tell who sang it

a recording or possibly   mass   was beginning

Then I saw a group of boys   kneeling at the altar

at the vase of red carnations   west of Teresa

They'd   entered with their staff   of priest

then   like a gust   departed

Teresa's dress is topography   a country

an architecture stone-made fluid like the skin

How will he pierce this infinite protection   the mind

created   to drift us from connection

The angel's wing will   draggle its song   will

trail in the wake of what's   recently wakened

Its melody   subdues   to the stress   of   Teresa's   folds

Her robe is an edge effect   it thrives   on abutment

like a stream soaks a pine root like   tide staining sand

like an arrow's nearness its   vertiginous   incipience

or two   groundswells: the angel   and Teresa

Or storm   systems   that startle at abutment

a clash then   entwinement   of barometric pressures

all the doubled instruments   of incidental   fury

Teresa and the angel form an existential   *happening*—

this is what Irving   Lavin once said

I love this notion   of chance in carved marble

unfettering the seam   between watcher   and creator

a febrile current   that ties my life to theirs   and theirs

to the pain that's always staining   our atmosphere

But how difficult   to sink

within a folded edge   effect—

to take up   my life   as a burrowing

light   so   strenuous to   plumb

the measured   place   his hand

will broach   her shoulder

I look so closely,   there are things I never see—

acanthus crowning   the pilaster   that gates her

the gold   cross hovering   to bisect   her robe

just at the summit of its compound   hillock—

and the prie-dieu   *dono Famiglia Scimonelli*

where I've never seen anyone   kneeling   to pray

Or how could I ignore Teresa's neighbor

St. Victoria lies in the crook across the way

Partially human in her transparent coffin

With preserved tooth butts and stitched sea-silk

And bone shard grafts and blood streaks her neck

And then I saw myself   in the Cornaro fathers

the Catholic elders who   commissioned   this work:

the rows of marble heads that Bernini   had sculpted

to watch Teresa   streaming in her theater...

all the fathers   are too busy to see her

they talk amongst themselves   turn

pages breathe   in each others' ears

I saw one gazing   with love into a column

his nose was nearly   pressing against it

how many columns   protect these men

from ecstasy: five, ten   I counted

more than   eighteen altogether

Some English-speaking students came

to visit Teresa on a Friday afternoon

pointing and squinting   taking

phones   from backpacks

Scribbled all over   with clothes

dye   tattoos   skin   hair

glitter   ribbon glitter   sneakers:

as soon as they lit   like moths

they were gone   *Are you inspired*

one had said   *I have   an idea*

A woman   took a selfie   with a flashcard: EK-STASIS

She was smiling in front of Teresa and the angel

To stand outside yourself she was pleased to illustrate

Teresa was   wallpaper   a primer   behind her

But doesn't every photograph   risk   violation

I did it myself   I'm sure   with my angles—

I caught her face once   at the bottom of the frame

flown from her body   from the angel's anchor

It sank   in a sea of porphyry columns

a softening   lotus   adrift in decoration

Or the day I looked through our old field glasses

I crawled on the magnified   fold the angel plucked

I was a voyeur   a shovel   of vision

Or maybe a spider on Bernini's marble

And one day I noticed

the angel's indirection ~   his arrow points

outward, away from Teresa's heart   His wrist

too delicate   to stay instrumental

Or maybe it's the skin   of the world

that will   puncture

Can I slope this way   unanchored   to sensation   my
cloak lit up like a runway   at night   my folds transporting
the flash of neural jewel   piercing and I flow away in
rivers   unto stars

This how I always knew   covering   was sensuous   its inner
lining   a hub   against the nerves

And yearning is an ancient thing   yearning has a skin

When I feel it   it carries   from the nipple roof throat
my self no longer   local   occurrence

my head like a beach like   riparian sanctity

but each toe   finger stays   taut with dissolution

When I want   something someone I can

feel it in my throat   then down

to a nipple   then descending   still

as I felt the organ's   reverberation

sink   against my skin last night

it tangled my left hip   could

cultivate   my edges

I made of myself   a radio   tower   to receive

right dissonance and   then   *legato* closure   —

I loved that distance   between near-noise and melody

my risen   expectation   that the phrase would have to end

Everywhere across   my body's   surfaces

tessellated mordents   looped long sound

like a   blank pearl series   or pulses in a wound

But in its slight   contraction

Teresa's trunk   beams   just as a lighthouse

fingers   a ship to port   a   clutch the

thatching   muscle under clothes

or the quicksilver   transfer

in dancers' *pas de deux*   that measures

captures   shares   deploys the

two dancers'   weight   : just as Teresa

carves   her trunk into an arch

bowlike   she   launches deepens

twirls   the arrow   in herself

She loves   the piercing

she truncates   his hips

the torrents of her   clothes

are shielding   his knees

his right hand holds the arrow

like a violin's   neck   to continue   :

the metaphor: she   is the conductor

How delicate   frenetic her silent

entropy   the currents   ranging

in the chaos   of her clothing

And she hopes   her body   will empty

its organs   will   whittle a membrane

the thinnest   shell for God

the roof   of my mouth

has thrown   a staircase to

a higher plane   or maybe

a *piano,*   if I translate

to Italian   (and so in my

English   a floor

must have a song)   The small

architectures   building

my anatomy   are melody

clusters   you find

in a basil leaf / *basilica*

I wanted   to rise with Teresa and the angel

to make   an errant   ending of my sight

but suddenly everything I saw   canted lateral:

the nub of their meeting   (hand   knee   fold)

was paving   a road within   the earthiness of earth

his arrow lengthened   to a measure of equator

a fulcrum   to magnetize and   scarify their corner

And then I saw   his right hand   better than I

ever had   his fingers half-closed but

open   like a writing   hand: a plume

or a pencil she'd   braid into her skin

and gravity   hugged them   as a tour

continued   behind me   in Spanish

On what I knew would be   my last day with Teresa

someone left a panda pillow   just outside

the church door   No one was sitting there

The person   had departed

And just inside   the darkened church

I saw Teresa's image   on a small red flyer

announcing   a lecture   on three

saints' lives   I leaned in   closer,

learned   that none of them   was hers

Like a montage of what I renounced   or loved

All I see is *repeat   repeat   repeat*

Every   swarm in her body   I'd record

The dangled   foot   susurration   inhale

A cloudlike system   banking   or failing

I know there is no new   knowledge or sensation

But everything escapes into a tree   unto metaphor

Stamped unto my eye

their two-leafed   body

alive now living   far from me

a petal   then two   within

an iris   opening

its ruffled   courier

lifting   slightly the   light

so far from me

NOTE

Most quotations in *The Right Hand* are attributed to their sources in the poems. The book also contains italicized lines from William Shakespeare, Marie de France, Richard Crashaw, Robert Frost, René Descartes, and St. Teresa of Avila.